BECKY MILLNER

MY PUPPY IS BORN

by Joanna Cole
with photographs
by Jerome Wexler

WILLIAM MORROW AND COMPANY
New York 1973

children's choice®

this book belongs
to

_____

A Children's Choice® Book Club Edition From Scholastic Book Services

Guess what?

The dog next door
is having puppies.
And I'm getting one!

There are lots of puppies
inside her.
Soon they will be born.
I can hardly wait.

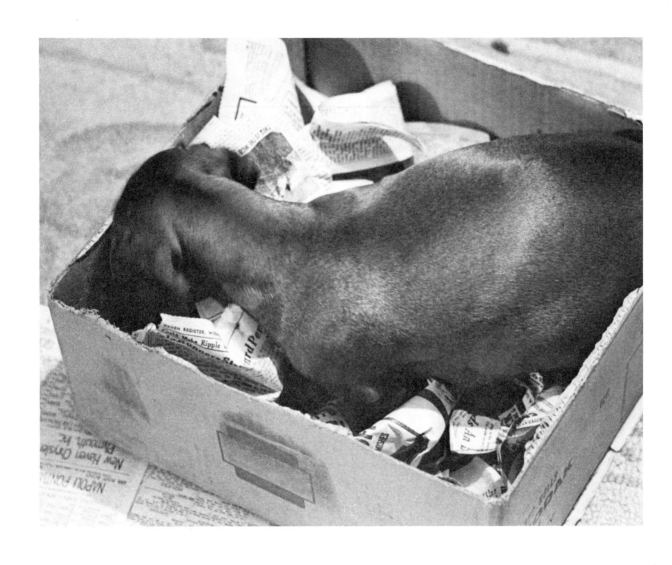

When the day arrives,
the mother dog goes to her box.
She tears up the papers
to make a soft nest.

The mother dog's muscles work hard
to push the first puppy out.

The first puppy comes.

It is born inside a sac.

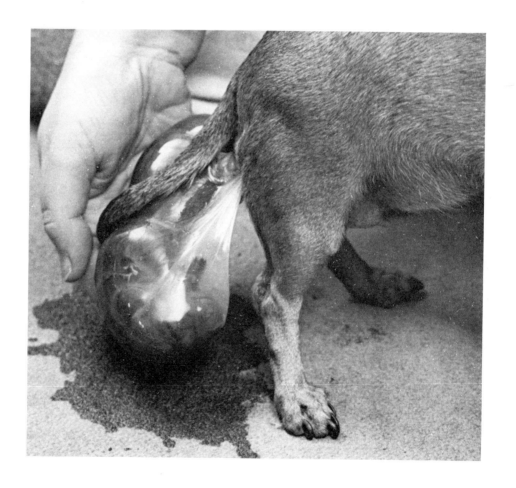

The mother dog tears the sac open
with her teeth.

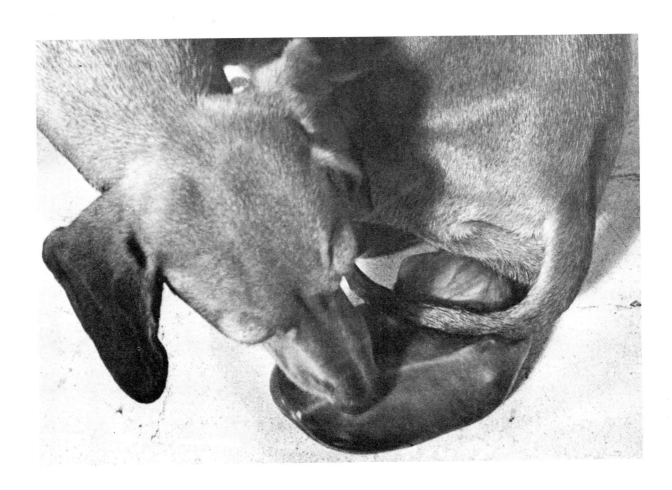

Now you can see the newborn puppy.
It is attached to its mother by a tube
called the "umbilical cord."
Before the puppy was born,
it got food and oxygen through this cord.

The mother has bitten through the cord.
Now the puppy must eat and breathe for itself.

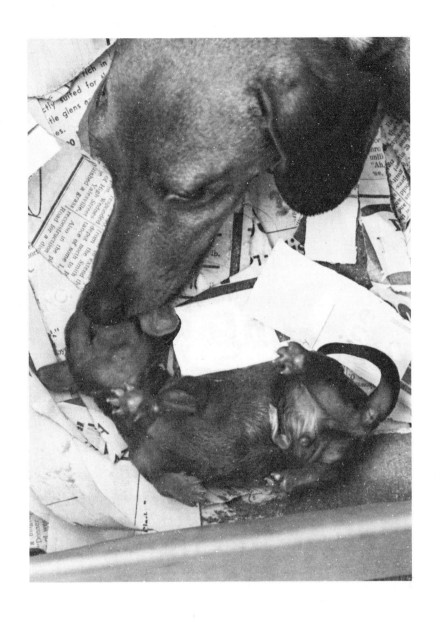

She licks and licks the puppy
until it is clean and dry.

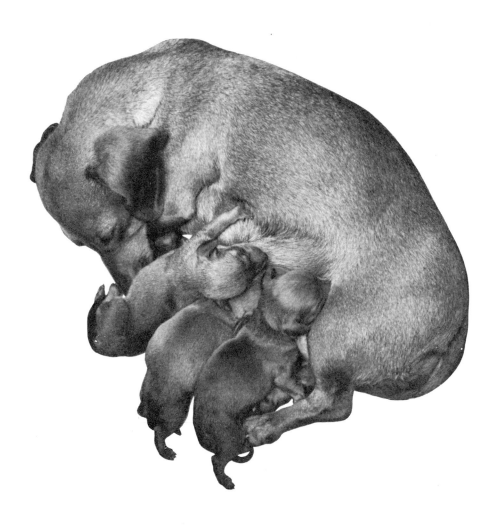

At last all the puppies are born.
The mother dog stays close to them.
She lets them nurse.
She keeps them clean.
She makes sure her babies
have plenty of peace and quiet.

The puppies are *all* wonderful.
But I have decided
this one is going to be mine.
His name is Sausage.

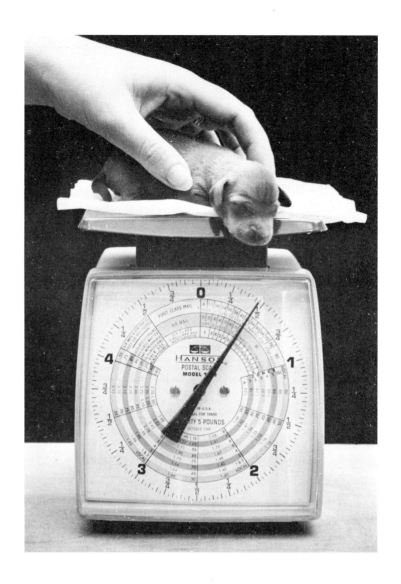

Sausage is very small.
He doesn't weigh much—
only a few ounces.

He can't see. His eyes won't open.
He can't hear either. His ears are plugged.

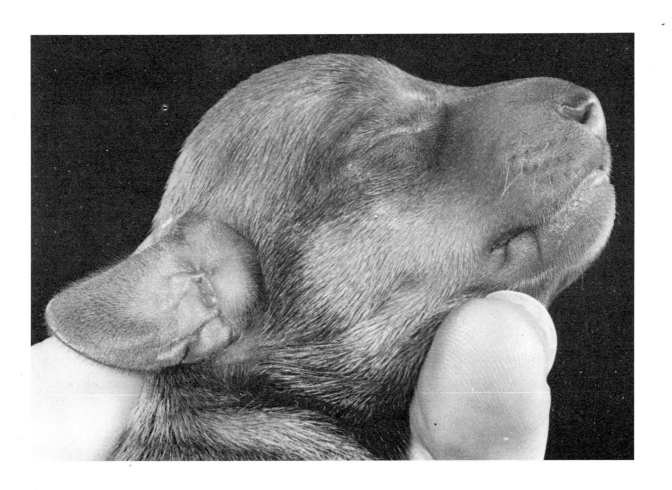

He is too weak to walk. He can only crawl.
He can't eat food. He has no teeth.

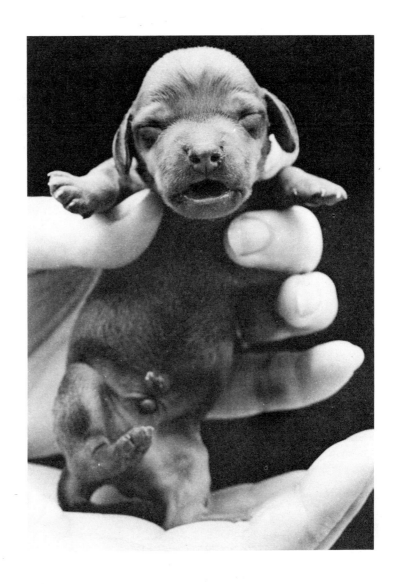

But he *can* make noise.
If you take him away from his mother,
he starts to cry.

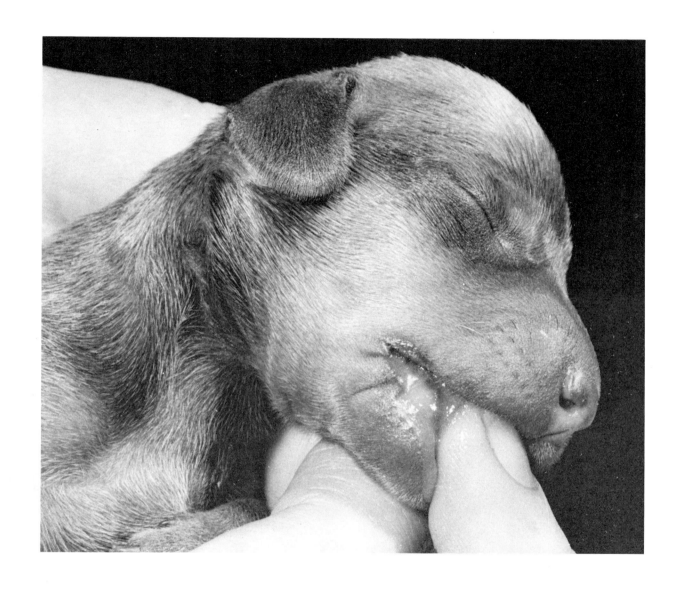

And he knows how to nurse already.
If you put your finger in his mouth,
he starts to suck.

When his mother is near,
he crawls to her.
He finds a nipple
and starts sucking milk.

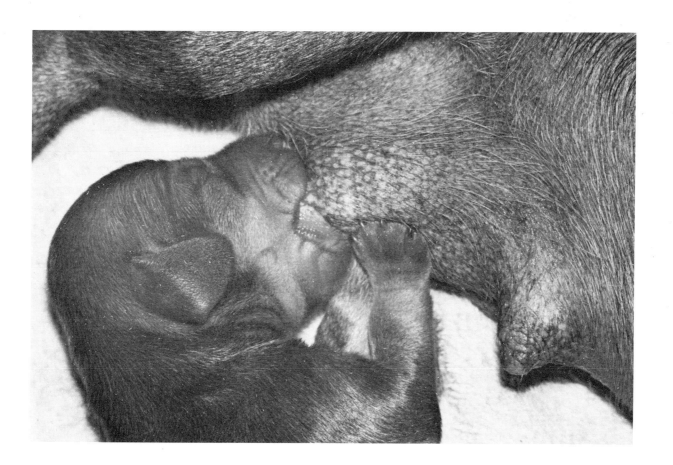

Every day Sausage grows.
He is two weeks old now.
His eyes are open.

His ears are open too.

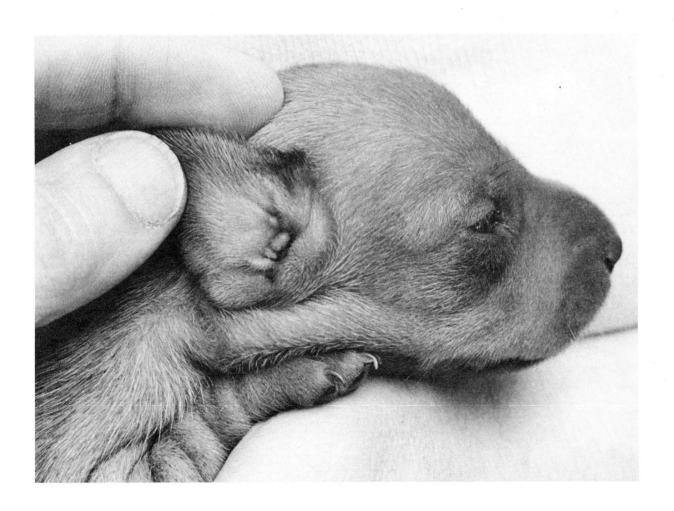

He is a lot bigger,
but he is still too weak to walk.

I want to play with my puppy,
but all he wants to do
is eat and sleep.
He is busy growing,
so I leave him alone.

As the weeks go by,
Sausage gets stronger.
Now he can sit up.
He seems happy about that.
Look at him howling!

Soon he takes his first step.

See?
Teeth!

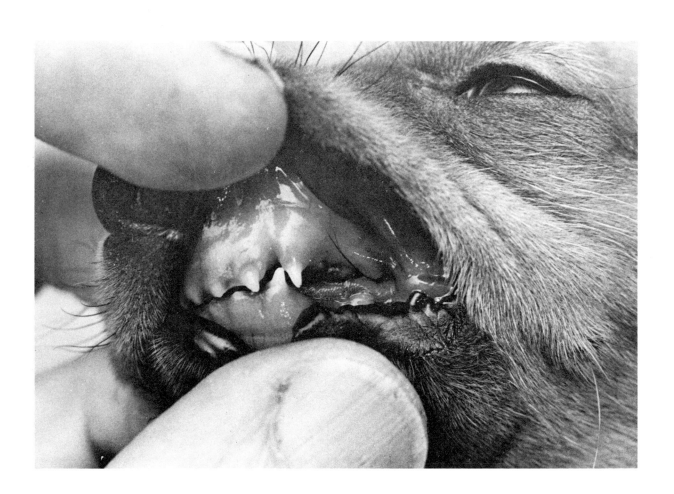

The puppies' new teeth hurt their mother.
She will not let them nurse as much.
Sausage doesn't like food at first.

But he gets used to it fast.

The puppies learn to eat
more and more solid food.

They learn to stay alone more.

They start to explore the world.

Sausage is the first one
to get out of the box by himself.

The puppies learn to play.
They play with their mother.

They play with other grown-up dogs.
They play together.

When Sausage is eight weeks old,
he is ready to leave his mother.
I got him a leash, but he doesn't like it.
At first he won't come.

But finally he follows me.

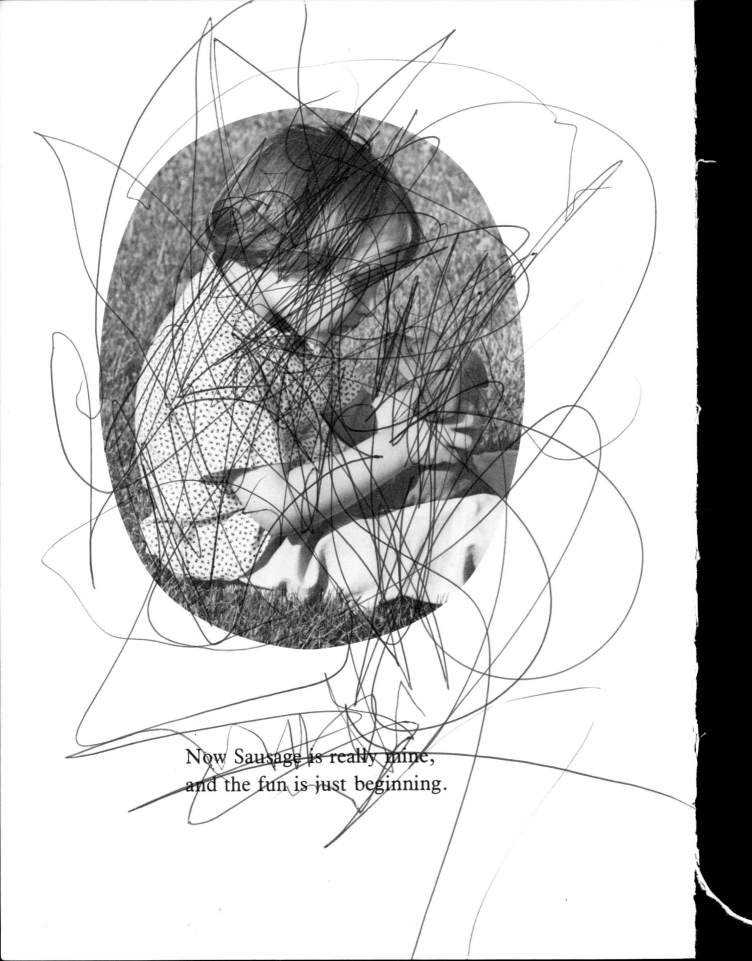

Now Sausage is really mine,
and the fun is just beginning.